children of the TITANIC

Christine Welldon

NIMBUS
PUBLISHING

Nimbus Publishing Limited
3731 Mackintosh St, Halifax, NS B3K 5A5
(902) 455-4286 nimbus.ca

Printed and bound in Canada
NB0981

Cover image: Original painting by marine artist Yves Bérubé, www.marineartgallery.com
Cover and interior design: Andrew Herygers

Library and Archives Canada Cataloguing in Publication

Welldon, Christine
Children of the Titanic / Christine Welldon.
ISBN 978-1-55109-892-0

1. Titanic (Steamship)—Juvenile literature. 2. Shipwrecks—North Atlantic Ocean—Juvenile literature. I. Title.

G530.T6W45 2012 j910.9163'4 C2011-907613-6

Communities, Culture and Heritage

The Canada Council | Le Conseil des Arts
for the Arts | du Canada

Nimbus Publishing acknowledges the financial support for its publishing activities from the Government of Canada through the Canada Book Fund (CBF) and the Canada Council for the Arts, and from the Province of Nova Scotia through the Department of Communities, Culture and Heritage.

Author's note:

The individual characters and stories portrayed in this work are entirely fictional and have no connection with any individuals or persons, living or dead. However the situations and experiences presented by the author are based on detailed historical research and, although time and personalities have been juxtaposed for the sake of exposition, every attempt has been made to share with the reader the nature and quality of the actual events at the time.

"I was only seven but I remember thinking everything in the world was standing still."

Eva Hart, survivor

Table of Contents

CHAPTER ONE

All Aboard!

How many words can you think of that mean huge? Enormous, gigantic, gargantuan...

TI-TAN-IC! The word "titanic" comes from the Titans, a family of gods who were huge, strong, powerful, and hard to beat. The ship, RMS *Titanic,* was all of these things, except for one—it was not hard to beat. It took two years and fifty thousand

Surpassing the Greatest Buildings and Memorials of Earth

The Largest and Finest Steamers in the World ☆ "OLYMPIC" AND "TITANIC"

White Star Line's New Leviathans ☆ 882½ Feet Long 92½ Feet Broad 45,000 Tons

The length of the *Titanic* **was greater than many of the tallest buildings on earth at that time.**

people to build the ship, and only two hours and one iceberg to sink it. It was a tragedy that wrecked thousands of lives.

One hundred and nine children, with their parents or guardians, boarded the *Titanic* when it began its first voyage in April 1912. Some families boarded with first-class tickets, others with second- or third-class. Some children

It took two years and more than fifty thousand people to build the *Titanic*.

were only babies, but many more children were old enough to explore the great ship and appreciate its wonders.

There were children who stayed with their wealthy parents in the grand first-class **staterooms**[1], exercised in the gymnasium and swimming pool, ate their meals in the sparkling dining hall, and played **quoits** on the covered decks.

1. Check the Glossary on page 86 for definitions of all the words you see in blue!

OLYMPIC AND TITANIC
EACH 45,000 TONS

WHITE STAR LINE

A pamphlet advertises the great ship *Titanic* and its sister ship, the *Olympic*.

Children whose parents held second-class tickets were able to roam decks that were open to the sky, and explore the great ship as far as they could go. Their staterooms were not as plush as first class on the *Titanic,* but their living quarters could easily pass for first class on any other ship.

Immigrant children and grown-ups down in **steerage** could not explore beyond the locked gates

Children could play on decks that were open to the sky.

that kept them from the decks above, but they and their parents were thrilled to stay in cabins with hot and cold running water, and electric lights. Although there were no sheets, there were comfortable mattresses and blankets in the bunk beds and their dining room offered food that was plain but plentiful.

10:00 A.M. WEDNESDAY, APRIL 10, 1912
Six-year-old Beth Cook clutched her doll tightly and looked up, up at the great ship with its four **funnels**

Titanic's four funnels seemed to touch the sky.

that seemed to touch the sky. Giant cranes held trunks and boxes suspended over the ship and crewmen steered them into the hold. She knew one of those trunks belonged to her family. There came a blast of ship's horns and she felt her Aunt Sara's hand on her back, gently guiding her toward the third-class gangway. Ahead of them, a man in uniform holding a clipboard called a greeting and asked for their names and tickets. As he looked at his list, the ship's doctor asked Sara some questions about their health. Then the crewman pointed down the long passageway.

"Cabin G137. G deck is that way. Turn right and follow the signs. Another steward will direct you from

Children of the Titanic

there." He bent down to talk to Beth. "What's your dolly's name?" he asked.

"Eliza," whispered Beth.

"Eliza, eh?" he said with a twinkle. "Well, look after her and make sure she doesn't get into any mischief."

He turned to greet the next group of people, and Beth followed her aunt along passageways to the narrow third-class cabin with an upper and lower **berth** where they were to sleep every night for the next seven nights.

"We'll get you and Eliza to bed, young lady," said Aunt Sara. "A little nap will do you no harm after such a long train ride."

Aunt Sara found Beth's nightdress in the suitcase they had brought, then tucked

In 1912, dolls like Eliza were made of porcelain and dressed like ladies.

her into her cozy bed. The hum of the great engines soon lulled her to sleep.

12:00 NOON, MONDAY, APRIL 10, 1912

Master John Crosby, eleven years old, read the sign, *No Passengers Beyond This Point,* and stepped past it. He opened a heavy door marked **Boiler** Room and peered inside. John felt hot steamy heat on his face and sticky **coal** dust in his nostrils. Men with grime on their faces and bare to the waist shovelled coal into the furnaces that raged and roared like hungry beasts, and in the background came a constant rumble as if the earth were opening. John gazed around him in wonder at the sheer height of the ceilings, the pipes and balconies and switchboards that surrounded him.

"Here, you!" A soot-faced worker with a shovel in his hands strode toward John. "This is off-limits, boy! Get back where you came from or I'll throw you off the ship."

John could scarcely hear the man's words over the noise of the machinery, but he didn't need a second warning. He ducked out the door, ran down the passageway, and climbed up the long

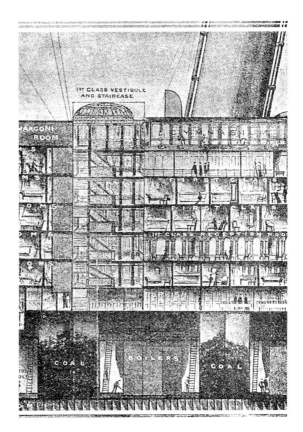

Stokers down in the hold worked around the clock shovelling coal into the ship's furnaces.

steep ladder to E deck. He was soon lost in a maze of hallways. A steward led him back into first class where passengers and visitors, dressed in their fine clothes, toasted each other with glasses of champagne to celebrate the start of the voyage. The ship's horns blasted and those friends who had come aboard to

A twenty-four-hour job

There were 29 boilers and 159 furnaces in the *Titanic* hold. Workers, called "**stokers**" or "**firemen,**" worked around the clock, shovelling coal into the furnaces. The men worked in shifts in a space that was very hot, at least 37°C.

"Trimmers" were men who shifted piles of coal to the boilers, using wheelbarrows. Trimmers and stokers were known as the "black gang"— their faces and bodies were covered with soot and coal dust.

say their last goodbyes streamed down the gangway. John could hear the faint music of a band playing. For all the noise, it was almost peaceful here, compared to the fury in the ship's hold.

John was used to luxury. His father had made a fortune in steel and the Crosby family always travelled in style, but the *Titanic* was the most luxurious ship John had ever sailed in. The swimming pool was fun, and so was the mechanical horse in the gym, but he had a hungry curiosity about the ship and a yearning to explore. He knew he would go back into the hold to watch and learn. They couldn't keep him away!

1:00 P.M. THURSDAY, APRIL 11, 1912

Charlotte Murphy had never in all her eight years seen a ship so big as the *Titanic*. She and her mother

Children of the Titanic

First- and second-class passengers enjoyed the ship's gymnasium with its mechanical horse.

and father waited with other families to board at Queenstown, Ireland, and start the journey across the Atlantic. They were leaving Ireland forever and when they arrived in New York they would take a train to Manitoba, Canada, where they would begin their new life. Along with all her clothes, she had been allowed to pack three of her favourite things in the family's big trunk. She had chosen pieces of her dollhouse furniture and wrapped them in some of her sewing

Differences

In Europe, there was a social class system of rich and poor. If you were born into the lower classes, you earned very little, and your plain clothing and speech told others that you were from the lower class. Middle-class people had earned their money through work in the trades, such as business or mines. They had enough to live very comfortably if they kept working. Upper-class people, known as the ruling class, usually inherited money and material possessions that allowed them to enjoy fine clothing and homes.

samplers. Her father had promised to craft another dollhouse when they reached their new home. There wasn't room for her hoop and stick, but instead, she chose an inlaid ivory jewel box that her grandmother had given her. It might be a long time before she saw her grandmother again.

They took one of the two small **tenders**, filled with passengers and mail bags, and were ferried to the *Titanic*, where it waited for them in deep water. Little boats followed along full of peddlers selling lace and other trinkets, hoping to attract the wealthier passengers on board.

Lottie and her parents boarded the ship and **stewards** directed them to follow the signs toward

Passengers with second-class tickets enjoyed luxurious staterooms.

second class on E deck. Lottie held tight to her mother's hand so she wouldn't become separated from her in the crush of people.

"But surely this is too grand to be ours?" asked her mother as they entered their

On Schedule

The RMS *Titanic* left the port of Southampton, England, on April 10th and sailed for Cherbourg, France, to pick up and drop off passengers. It sailed on to Queenstown, Ireland, so that more people could embark, then, on April 11th, began its journey across the Atlantic toward New York City.

Passengers in second class enjoyed the same menu as those in first class.

cabin for the first time. There was a fine carpet, comfortable sleeping berths, a sink with hot and cold running water, and a wardrobe where they could hang their clothes. While Lottie's mother unpacked their things, her father led her on a tour of the middle-class deck. A harmonica player played a merry tune as they walked along, and she could hear music coming from one of the upper decks.

Lottie and her father called hello to other passengers as they explored the dining room where

The *Titanic* is launched at Belfast in May 1911.

they would have all their meals together, the electric elevator, the barber shop, and the sitting rooms. She couldn't wait to read some of the books in the library and sit in the plush armchairs in the reading room. Then came three blasts of the ship's horns.

"Come on, Lottie. Let's go and wave goodbye to Ireland," said her father. "We'll be leaving very soon."

They went out on deck, and as a passenger played an Irish jig on the bagpipes, they gazed at the shores of their home country, its green hills vivid in the

A LAST VISION OF THE "TITANIC" BY NIGHT—AN IMPRESSION AT CHERBOURG

The "Titanic" after sailing from Southampton put in at Cherbourg to pick up her European passengers. This view gives a very good impression of the vessel during her one and only visit to the French port on the evening of Wednesday, April 10. Her hundreds of portholes produced a kind of shimmering glow upon the darkness of the surrounding water.

The *Titanic* as it left Cherbourg on its way to Ireland.

sunshine. Lottie waved goodbye to this country she loved. The distance between ship and shore widened, and Ireland seemed to shrink as they sailed farther away. Their journey had begun.

Children of the Titanic

CHAPTER TWO

A Ship's Tour

The water was calm. *Titanic* passengers, lulled by the motion of the ship on their first day at sea, lazed in deck chairs or explored. There was the smell of new paint and freshly varnished decks, the excited buzz of small children, and the ever-present horizon where sea and sky met.

What was it like for the passengers on board the *Titanic*? Most of the young children and babies in first class had nurses and nannies to take care of them. Adults in first class spent much of their time dressing for breakfast, dinner, and supper, and they changed clothes at least four times each day! Between the first and second of the four funnels was a grand staircase enclosed by a domed glass ceiling. It led to the gymnasium, a swimming pool, **Turkish bath**, smoking room, library, and a French café. Children could enjoy games in the gym or the children's nursery, swim in the pool, or play deck quoits. Their parents might exercise on the gym's mechanical camel and punching bag, play a game of squash, or puff on cigars and cigarettes in the smoking room.

Life in second class, though full of luxuries, was not so formal. Passengers did not change clothes four times each day. They could not use the Turkish bath but they could enjoy the gym, and their area of the ship might easily be mistaken for first class on any other ship.

The *Titanic* and her sister ship, the *Olympic*, were the two largest ships ever built at that time.

As for those in steerage, the White Star Line wanted the experience of third-class passengers and their children to be comfortable, because most were on their way to a new land and new lives. Down in the hold were the narrow cabins of these immigrant families. All were seeking a new life in the United States

The Reading Room in first class was a comfortable place to spend some time.

or Canada. By law, they were not allowed to leave the lower part of the ship and there were locked gates and barriers to keep them in their own area. They and their children gathered either in the General Room or on a corner of C deck; meeting places where they could talk, and play lively music or games.

The sweeping grand staircase was a remarkable feature of the *Titanic*.

10:00 A.M., FRIDAY, APRIL 12

Lottie stood with her father on the **promenade** deck
and waited for the Captain to appear. A morning
bulletin, slipped under their cabin door, had informed

them that the Captain always began his ship's inspection at 10:00 A.M. He toured the ship, from top to bottom, **fore** to **aft**, to make sure everything was in working order.

Lottie's mother was nervous about sailing on the *Titanic.* "I have a funny feeling about this ship," Lottie heard her saying. "They say it is unsinkable but that is inviting disaster." She was sure it was going to sink and that it would happen at night. Lottie's father laughed and asked his wife how the biggest, safest ship in the world could ever sink. But Lottie's mother was certain of it.

Last night she had sat up late knitting and reading, then went to breakfast with Lottie, and now she was going to bed. She planned to sleep late into the afternoon. She wanted to be ready for an emergency at night, just in case.

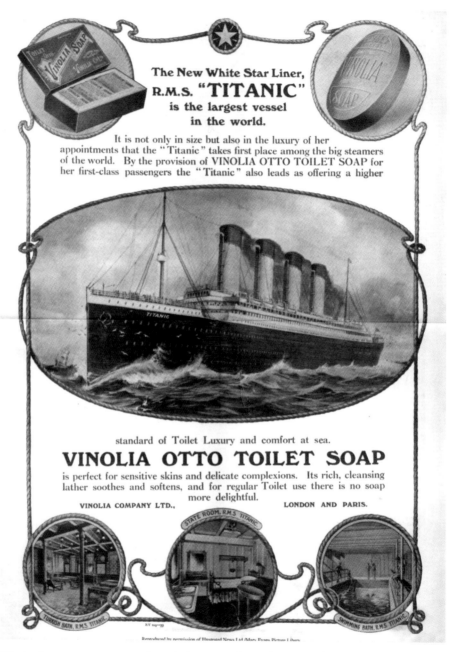

The New White Star Liner,
R.M.S. "TITANIC"
is the largest vessel
in the world.

It is not only in size but also in the luxury of her appointments that the "Titanic" takes first place among the big steamers of the world. By the provision of VINOLIA OTTO TOILET SOAP for her first-class passengers the "Titanic" also leads as offering a higher

standard of Toilet Luxury and comfort at sea.

VINOLIA OTTO TOILET SOAP

is perfect for sensitive skins and delicate complexions. Its rich, cleansing lather soothes and softens, and for regular Toilet use there is no soap more delightful.

VINOLIA COMPANY LTD.,   LONDON AND PARIS.

First-class passengers enjoyed the most luxurious products. Here is a typical advertisement for an expensive soap used on the *Titanic*.

Children of the Titanic

The General Room was a lively place where parents and children in third class met for music, dancing, conversation, and play.

Lottie put on her best dress and her mother made sure her shoes were polished and her hair was neat. "Everything must be shiny on the *Titanic*," laughed Lottie's father. "Even the passengers!" Here they came—a group of officers led by Captain Smith were walking along the second-class promenade toward them. The Captain wore his uniform and all his medals. He sported a neatly trimmed white beard and mustache, and had a clear-eyed gaze and kind expression.

Captain "E. J."

Passengers and crew alike enjoyed sailing with Captain Edward J. Smith. He was a kind man, and many purposely chose to sail on ships that he captained because they trusted him to give them a safe passage. Known as "E. J." by passengers and crew, the Captain was admired and respected by all. The White Star Line usually placed him in command of any ship on its first voyage. At sixty-two years of age, Captain Smith planned to retire after this voyage on the *Titanic*.

"How do you do, Captain Smith," said her father, stepping out to greet him. Captain Smith asked how they were enjoying the voyage. He smiled at Lottie.

"I have a daughter not much older than you," he said to her. "She's at home with her mother, not as lucky as you are."

Children of the Titanic

Lottie smiled back at this tall man as he bent to shake her hand.

"Well, I must carry on with my day's work," he said. He saluted her, and Lottie watched them go. She thought he must be a very busy and important man to be in charge of this great ship. She was glad he had time to stop and say hello.

11:30 A.M. SATURDAY, APRIL 13

The floor shook with lively dance steps and Beth clapped her hands in time with the music. Everyone in steerage class loved to gather in the General Room to play or listen to music, and talk. This morning, a tin whistler and a fiddler played together, and some passengers were dancing an Irish jig. The tunes reminded everyone of their home in the old country and gave them cheerful hopes about the new life they were sailing toward.

Beth was getting used to the ship. She liked their little cabin with the bunk beds and the wash basin. It was their home away from home for a few days. Last night she had awoken in the night and forgotten that she was not in her own little bed in England. She called out for her mother, but then she remembered that her mother was still in London where she worked as an actress in the theatre.

It would be a few months before she saw her mother again. Beth and her aunt were going to stay in New York for a while and then her mother would come across the ocean to join them.

At breakfast that morning, she sat with her aunt in the dining room at the long tables beside other parents and children. There were a few Irish children, but many of the children spoke in languages she had never heard before. She managed to talk to them anyway, using gestures and smiles, and they seemed to understand. She was glad to see the porridge and milk that she liked so much. Dinner was at noon, and her aunt said she was looking forward to the roast beef and boiled potatoes.

Now, everyone in steerage class was gathered here in the General Room to pass the time.

A white-haired man in uniform waved hello to them from the doorway.

"That's Captain Smith, on his ship's tour," said her aunt. "He has the most important job on board."

He looked very important, too, but he did have a smile for everyone.

Some little girls skipped past Beth, in time with the music, and she ran after them and joined in their games.

3:00 P.M. SATURDAY, APRIL 13

The wailing music of bagpipes and the cheerful tunes of the tin whistle were the first thing John had heard after breakfast that morning as he stood on the **boat deck**. He had peered over the railing to see where the sounds were coming from, and could see a corner of C deck, where third-class passengers laughed and danced. He had been curious about these men and women ever

A Fake Funnel

The *Titanic* had four funnels. The first three funnels vented smoke and fumes from the ship's boiler room but the fourth funnel was a fake. It was there to make the ship look more powerful and balanced. However, it did have piping connected to the ship's cooking stoves and helped to vent the **galley** of any fumes from cooking.

The menu in third class was very basic compared to first and second class, but the food was plentiful.

since he'd watched them boarding the ship in Southampton. It had been easy to pick them out that first day as they walked up a gangway that led into the hold. They were plainly dressed and some carried their belongings in cloth bags clutched in their hands or in bundles on their backs.

His father told him that there were many nationalities on board the ship: Italians, Russians, Irish, Germans, Swedes, and others, all leaving their home country behind. He noticed their anxious expressions at the time, but ever since then, they'd been having lots of fun, much more than the first-class passengers.

The ship's crew used steep iron ladders as shortcuts from one deck to the next. John had climbed up and down a few and knew where some of them led. He climbed down a ladder that led from second class to third, and walked along a hallway towards the sound of the music. He noticed some open doors that revealed tiny cabins with bunk beds so much smaller than his **parlour suite**. At the doors of the General Room, he stopped and looked in. Groups of men stood around the large room talking loudly, children darted here and there, playing tag, women sat on wooden benches and tended to their babies, a man with a harmonica played in one corner and several men and women danced to the merry tunes. John stood watching for some minutes until a few people turned to stare at him. They knew he was not one of them by his finer clothing. "Come in!" shouted one of the men with sparkling eyes. "Join us!"

John smiled and shook his head, feeling suddenly shy. He waved goodbye and went on his way, but soon became lost. There seemed to be miles of passageways and dead ends, a maze that was hard to navigate until a crew member showed him the way back, unlocking a gate that led to an upper deck. He thought about the steerage class passengers he had seen. They might be poor, but they didn't seem to have a care in the world.

CHAPTER THREE

Life on Board

The time on board passed quickly. By Sunday, April 14th, the *Titanic* was steaming west by southwest and entering the cool waters of the Labrador current. In two more days, they would reach New York. Because it was the second-last night on board, first-class passengers would wear their finest clothes for dinner. The women laid out the evening gowns they had been saving for just this last formal meal on board. The men would wear white tie and tails.

About one hundred passengers gathered around the piano in the second class dining room for a hymn sing after dinner. People called out their choices and many of the hymns described the dangers of travelling by sea.

How Many?

There were 325 passengers in first class, 285 in second class, and 706 in third class. Of these, 109 were children. In total, there were 2,223 people including the crew. The *Titanic* carried 20 lifeboats, enough for only 1,178 people. There were 3,500 lifebelts and 48 life rings. It was believed that the *Titanic* was so well built that it would never sink.

The library was a cozy place to be, especially on colder evenings.

They sang a special hymn, "For Those in Peril on the Sea," in hushed voices.

Steerage passengers were getting ready for a dance in the General Room, when a large rat ran across the floor and some children screamed while others chased it.

The crew was warned to watch out for icebergs. The outside temperature was ten degrees colder than yesterday, so they were expecting some ice. "Keep a sharp lookout, especially for small bergs and

Children of the Titanic

growlers," they told each other in the **crow's nest**.

The sea was very smooth, so there would be no white wavelets smacking the bottom of the bergs to give away their position. Someone had taken the binoculars from the crow's nest and not returned them. The two crew members on night watch had to do without. Their eyesight was not very good. They stared into the moonless night.

Taking baths

While some first-class passengers had private bathrooms in their suite of rooms, there were many shared bathrooms in first and second class. In steerage class, there were only two bathrooms. This was not a concern for many. At that time, many people believed that taking baths was bad for their health.

4:30 P.M. SUNDAY, APRIL 14

Beth heard the gong that signalled tea time in the dining room. There was to be a hymn sing afterwards, because today was Sunday.

Beth had already made many friends and learned some new games. The skipping rope game was a little hard for her short legs, but she loved to race with the other girls and learn their skipping songs. On her first day, she took her doll, Eliza, for a tour along the hallways and decks, the dining room and meeting room, but later she began to leave her in the cabin. Eliza was just too big to carry everywhere.

Aunt Sara said she was glad it was so calm at sea. No one was seasick yet, because the ocean was very flat and smooth. Beth and her aunt liked to watch the sun set every evening. The skies were clear and the sun was like a great ball of flame leaving a golden path along the sea.

6:00 P.M. SUNDAY, APRIL 14

This evening it was much colder outside, so before supper Lottie sat in the cozy library with her father and some others. They were filling out immigration forms so they would be ready to go through customs in New York. That meant only two more nights on this ship, then it was to be a brand new world for Lottie and her family.

Lottie was getting used to the vibration of the ship, especially at night when she went to bed. It was a gentle motion that she hardly felt unless she

Children of the Titanic

paid attention to it. The ship was speeding along, leaving white foam in its wake, and her father said that at this rate, they might even reach New York by Tuesday night instead of Wednesday morning.

Lottie heard the gong for dinner. "Go and ask your mother to come along to the dining room," said her father. Her mother was resting late every day, because she sat up at night, listening for changes in the sound of the engines.

John Jacob Astor was the wealthiest passenger on the *Titanic*, with a fortune of over $2 billion in today's dollars.

Lottie had heard her say she was sure there was going to be a disaster, but her father had hushed her.

Lottie couldn't believe that anything could go wrong on this ship. It was as big as a city, and she felt very safe walking along the deck or sitting in the library. Even so, whenever she saw her mother's fear, she felt a tiny worry.

9:00 P.M. SUNDAY, APRIL 14

John was always free to wander wherever he liked on the ship. His father had brought paperwork with him and left John to find his own entertainment. John and some new friends had played squash in the gym, swum in the swimming pool filled with fresh sea water, and eaten two and sometimes three desserts at every meal.

John read the menu for that night. There was to be roast beef, lamb, duckling, and for dessert, John's favourite: chocolate éclairs and ice cream.

The church service was cancelled that

R.M.S. "TITANIC."

APRIL 14, 1912.

HORS D'ŒUVRE VARIÉS
OYSTERS

CONSOMMÉ OLGA   CREAM OF BARLEY

SALMON, MOUSSELINE SAUCE, CUCUMBER

FILET MIGNONS LILI
SAUTÉ OF CHICKEN, LYONNAISE
VEGETABLE MARROW FARCIE

LAMB, MINT SAUCE
ROAST DUCKLING, APPLE SAUCE
SIRLOIN OF BEEF, CHATEAU POTATOES

GREEN PEAS   CREAMED CARROTS
BOILED RICE
PARMENTIER & BOILED NEW POTATOES

PUNCH ROMAINE

ROAST SQUAB & CRESS
COLD ASPARAGUS, VINAIGRETTE
PÂTE DE FOIE GRAS
CELERY

WALDORF PUDDING
PEACHES IN CHARTREUSE JELLY
CHOCOLATE & VANILLA ECLAIRS
FRENCH ICE CREAM

The last dinner on the *Titanic* offered a menu full of delicious choices for first-class passengers. They dressed in their finest clothes for this formal occasion.

Children of the Titanic

Morse Code

A	• ━	M	━ ━	Y	━ • ━ ━	6	━ • • • •
B	━ • • •	N	━ •	Z	━ ━ • •	7	━ ━ • • •
C	━ • ━ •	O	━ ━ ━	Ä	• ━ • ━	8	━ ━ ━ • •
D	━ • •	P	• ━ ━ •	Ö	━ ━ ━ •	9	━ ━ ━ ━ •
E	•	Q	━ ━ • ━	Ü	• • ━ ━	.	• ━ • ━ • ━
F	• • ━ •	R	• ━ •	Ch	━ ━ ━ ━	,	━ ━ • • ━ ━
G	━ ━ •	S	• • •	0	━ ━ ━ ━ ━	?	• • ━ ━ • •
H	• • • •	T	━	1	• ━ ━ ━ ━	!	• • ━ ━ •
I	• •	U	• • ━	2	• • ━ ━ ━	:	━ ━ ━ • • •
J	• ━ ━ ━	V	• • • ━	3	• • • ━ ━	"	• ━ • • ━ •
K	━ • ━	W	• ━ ━	4	• • • • ━	'	• ━ ━ ━ ━ •
L	• ━ • •	X	━ • • ━	5	• • • • •	=	━ • • • ━

Morse code was used to send messages from ship to ship, or from ship to shore.

evening, but after dinner John went to C deck to run an errand for his father. He left a written message at the inquiry office to be sent by **telegram** to the New York hotel where they would be staying. He watched as the crewman placed his message in a **pneumatic tube**. He knew it would travel up to the **Marconi** room on the boat deck and there, radio officers would tap out the message in Morse code, the short and long sounds of dots and dashes.

CHAPTER FOUR

Iceberg Right Ahead!

"Icebergs sighted," read one of several radio messages that the telegraphers on the *Titanic* received. The great ship steamed steadily on, even faster than usual. It was just before midnight and although the crew was on the watch for ice, Captain Smith was not worried. The *Titanic* had fifteen watertight compartments that ensured the ship would not sink if there were an accident and any two were flooded.

As they gazed out into the night, the crew saw something large and ominous looming in the waters ahead. A look-out crewman quickly tugged three times on the rope of the bronze bell overhead and spoke into the telephone beside him.

"Iceberg right ahead," he snapped to the **bridge** crew.

"Thank you," said the First Officer. "Hard to **starboard**."

In the crow's nest, the crewmen stared in horror at the berg that had crept up on them. They braced themselves for a head-on collision while

"Keep a sharp lookout for icebergs!"

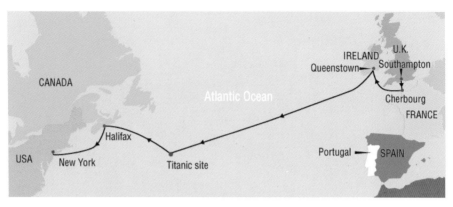

The *Titanic* entered a field of icebergs that littered the shipping lanes off Newfoundland's Grand Banks.

the **helmsman** on the bridge spun the ship's wheel as far as it would go. The prow slowly swung left. Everyone held their breath. Would they swing clear in time? Then came a jarring shudder. Large chunks of ice scattered over the foredeck. The underwater spur of the iceberg scraped down the starboard side of the **hull**. Over the pounding of the ice, the men could hear another sound. It was the sound of metal ripping. The 6th Officer stepped out onto the bridge deck. He could almost reach out and touch the berg as it passed by. It was a "blue" berg. It had turned over and was dark with sea water, and so had been hard to spot in the night, especially without binoculars.

Children of the Titanic

The officer on the bridge used the hand lever to close the watertight doors between the boiler rooms and ordered the engine room to stop engines. The engineers in the hold felt the collision and saw that water was beginning to flood into the boiler rooms. The stokers and firemen quickly jumped through the doorway into the next boiler room before the iron watertight door was closed by the bridge crew above. They had to hurry or they would be trapped inside. Water began to sweep across the boiler-room floors, one by one, as the sea thundered into the ship. The firemen were the first to realize that five of the ship's watertight compartments had been torn and were open to the sea.

Towers of Ice

Icebergs can rise one hundred metres into the air and reach down four hundred metres below sea level.

They were formed as many as twenty thousand years ago. Growlers, pieces that have broken away from the berg, litter the sea with large chunks that are dangerous to ships until they melt away. It takes an iceberg two years to drift from Baffin Bay to Newfoundland's Grand Banks.

The *Titanic* received warnings of field ice and bergs by Marconi telegraph throughout the day from other ships in the area.

A model wears a gown designed by Lady Lucile Duff-Gordon, a *Titanic* passenger. Lady Gordon probably wore one of her own high-fashion designs for her last dinner on board. She survived the sinking.

It was 11:40 P.M. On the lower decks, people hardly noticed the shudder of the ship. Most young children were asleep in their beds. The night chef in the ship's galley saw a pan of bread rolls tremble and fall to the floor. First-class passengers had just left a party in honour of Captain Smith and stood in the smoking room, chatting. Their talk stopped suddenly at the faint shuddering motion. A passenger in second class, getting ready for bed, was startled when chunks of ice fell through his open porthole. Some third-class passengers who were on deck played football with pieces of ice.

The ship's carpenter checked all over the ship for damage. He saw water covering the mail-room floor on F deck, as crew tried to rescue bags of mail. It would not be long before the sea flooded the entire ship. He brought this terrible news to the Captain.

"She's making water, fast!" he called, as he hurried up the bridge ladder. "She's going to sink!"

Captain Smith was living his worst fear as captain. He learned that in just over one hour the *Titanic* would sink to the ocean floor, and he knew that there were not enough lifeboats for everyone.

12:30 A.M. MONDAY, APRIL 15

John woke up. Something was wrong. He had felt a shudder as though the ship was being given a little push. Then there came a silence. There was no vibration of engines because the clothes in his wardrobe were not gently swaying as they always

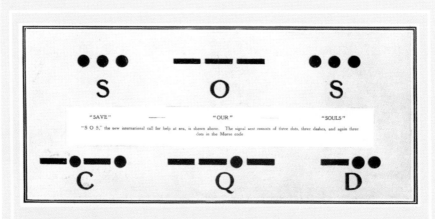

Morse Code

The first wireless message asking for help said: "*Titanic* sends *CQD*. Requires Assistance. Position 41 degrees 44'N Longitude 50 degrees 24'W. Come at once."

did. He drifted back into sleep for a while until voices in the passageway outside woke him.

Someone knocked on his door. "Have everyone come out to the boat deck, and wear your life jackets, sir," said a steward as John opened the door.

"What's happened?" he asked.

The steward was knocking on his father's stateroom door, next to John's. "Just a precaution. Nothing to worry about," he called.

Children of the Titanic

John went into his father's room through the connecting door to wake him.

"Something's happened," he called. "I'm going up to see."

"I'll come with you," said his father. They pulled on their clothes and the two made their way along the passageway toward the grand staircase. In the lounge, a group of musicians was playing and other passengers, some still dressed in their best evening clothes, strolled toward them, soothed by the music.

"We might have to cancel our squash game tomorrow," joked one.

John's father stood for several minutes, talking to his friends.

They knew the ship had collided with an iceberg but did not think they were in any danger. The *Titanic* could not sink.

A steward hurried past them. "Please get your life jackets and go to the boat deck," he said.

John and his father began to understand that the situation was serious. They hurried back down the grand staircase and onto the promenade deck. There,

Wealthy passengers could afford a suite of rooms with connecting doors.

a frightening scene met their eyes. Crowds of people stood on the deck. Children were crying, and women were calling out to their husbands and being ushered into a lifeboat. John heard scattered conversations, talk of an iceberg, and a hole in the ship's side.

"We'd better go back down to the stateroom for our life jackets," said John's father. "If we have to leave the ship, there are some papers I want to retrieve."

When they reached their stateroom, John's father gave him some important papers and money and told him to keep them safe.

"Is the *Titanic* really sinking?" asked John.

"Don't worry," said his father. "I heard a rescue ship is coming soon."

They put on extra clothes under their life jackets for warmth. It was 1:30 in the morning, but John felt wide awake now. He thought he heard the distant sound of gunshots. They walked up the grand staircase and the steps seemed to tilt under their feet. John held on to the railing to steady himself. On the boat deck, a lifeboat hung out at an angle to the ship and John could see the ship was much lower in the water and listing to one side. Women were climbing across deck chairs that bridged the gap between the ship and the lifeboat. A group of musicians stood nearby, playing waltz music.

"Women and children, first," called out a crewman as he lifted a little girl into the boat.

"In you go," said John's father firmly. "I'll follow later." John hesitated. He did not want to leave his father.

"I'll stay here with you," decided John, stepping back, but his father held out his hand to say goodbye.

John and his father saw a frightening scene.

"Help will come. Don't worry about me."

They shook hands, and John began to climb across the deck chair.

He was seized roughly by the shoulder. "Women and children only!" a crewman shouted.

His father protested. "Of course the boy goes. He is only eleven!"

Children of the Titanic

The crewman stepped aside and John climbed into the boat.

"No more boys!" he heard the man say.

John found a seat beside other children and mothers. He looked over to where he had last seen his father but couldn't find him in the crowd on deck. A girl wearing a woman's hat and shawl clambered into the boat. John recognized this child. It was not a girl, but his friend Ned in disguise. He was only thirteen years old, but even at that young age he was considered a man. If anyone noticed his disguise, Ned would be ordered out of the boat. John kept quiet and did not give him away.

An older boy, almost eighteen, made a rush for the boat and jumped in. No sooner had he found a seat than an officer in the boat held a gun to his face.

"Women and children only. You have ten seconds to get off this boat," he ordered.

The boy began to sob. "Please, let me stay." He looked very young to John; just a child.

"Be a man," said the officer in a quiet voice. "There are women and children to save."

The boy's eyes pleaded, but he crawled back onto the ship. John never saw him again.

There were six children in first class. Five were saved.

1:15 A.M. Monday, April 15

Lottie did not feel the bump when the ship collided. She was fast asleep, but her mother shook her awake and told her to get dressed quickly. She saw the fear in her mother's eyes and heard feet pounding on the deck above. She wondered if her mother had been right all along. Was the ship going to sink? Her father had already gone up to investigate. Her mother was dressed in her heavy coat and wearing her lifebelt. She put a lifebelt on over Lottie's coat, took a blanket, then led her up the staircase to the boat deck. There, people stood about, some wearing nightgowns and robes under their life jackets, or coats that had been flung on in a hurry over their night clothes.

It was frosty cold on deck. They saw Lottie's father through the crowds and pushed their way toward him.

"I want you both to be brave," he said. "The ship has collided with an iceberg and done some damage. A rescue ship is coming, but just to be safe, they want you to get into the lifeboat. We'll be back on the ship by morning, I'm sure."

"I won't go without my husband," said Lottie's mother.

An officer came over to the little family and told Lottie and her mother to go over to the lifeboats. There, two men stood at the side of a boat helping people to climb in.

"Women and children only," they called.

There was an explosion and a bright light lit the deck.

"It's the ship's rockets. They're calling other boats to pick us up," said Lottie's father.

He hugged them both, and said he would find them later.

A crewman lifted Lottie up and put her in the boat.

This iceberg was photographed in 1962, very close to the place where the *Titanic* sank.

Others tried to help her mother into the boat but she pushed them away.

"Not without my husband," she said.

"You must go now, Mary. There's Lottie to take care of. I'll be along, later," said her father.

Her mother hesitated, then climbed into the boat. Another rocket flared, and in the light, her face looked grim.

Lottie and her mother had scarcely sat down when three men rushed over the side and into the boat, almost crushing some passengers in the middle. An officer in the lifeboat fired his gun into the sky and told them to get out or he would shoot them. Lottie's mother screamed, "Don't shoot!" but the officer looked as though he meant it, and the men quickly climbed out of the boat.

"Daddy! Daddy!" cried Lottie. Why couldn't he get into the boat with them?

Crewmen hauled on the ropes to lower them, and the boat jerked this way and that, down, down into the water.

There were twenty-four children in second class. All were saved.

1:30 A.M. MONDAY, APRIL 15

"We have to get up," said Beth's aunt, gently shaking her awake. "Get dressed quickly." Beth opened her eyes. Her aunt was already dressed and wore a life jacket over her coat. A few minutes earlier, she had answered a knock on the door. One of the Irish passengers told her the ship was in trouble and she must try to reach the lifeboats. Sara helped the sleepy Beth to get dressed and put on her life jacket.

"Is it daytime?" asked Beth.

"Come along, child. No time for talking."

Beth could hear shouts outside the cabin door and hurrying footsteps. She slipped her feet into her shoes while her aunt opened the door. Outside the cabin, there were people everywhere, pushing their way to the staircase, talking excitedly. At the bottom of the staircase stood a big crowd of people, all trying to get up the stairs at once, talking and shouting in different languages. There was no room to move and the crowd tried to struggle and push their way up, but it was useless. There were just too many people.

Some crewmen on the second-class deck above leaned over the stairway and reached down for the women, pulling them up over the heads of the crowd. "Women and children!" they shouted over the din of voices. They reached for Beth's Aunt Sara, but she lifted Beth and held her as high as she could above her head.

"Reach out and take the kind man's hands," she told Beth.

"Step on my head, kiddie," said a man beside her. He lifted her up to stand on his head while he held

Children of the Titanic

her. He looked up to make sure she was being grasped by the crewman up above, and Beth had to step on his face. She didn't want to scratch him and she began to cry.

"Reach up!" shouted her aunt. Hands held Beth's, and she was hauled up to the deck above.

"Now, you, Miss," said the man to Sara. He helped to lift her and a crewman standing above bent

Into the Deep

As the bow submerged and the stern rose higher, the forward funnel broke loose in a shower of sparks and plunged down into the water among the frantic swimmers. The ship snapped in half between the third and fourth funnels. The stern stood up in the water for about five minutes, throwing those left on deck into the sea. Then it slipped down beneath the waves. The *Titanic* sank in two hours and forty minutes.

down to tug her up until she was standing beside Beth and some other women and children.

"Goodbye, Miss, and good luck," called the man below to her aunt.

The crewman urged this small group along and called to the other women and children to follow, but the women didn't understand what he was saying. They only knew a few words of English. They hung back with their children, talking excitedly in their own language, waiting for their husbands to come up onto the second-class deck from the crowd below.

Beth remembered her doll. "I forgot Eliza!" she wailed, but there was too much noise and no one was listening.

There were seventy-nine children in third class. Twenty-seven were saved.

CHAPTER FIVE

Women and Children First

Why should they leave the comfortable ship to step into a little boat tossing in the ocean? Many first- and second-class passengers refused to board the lifeboats, but when at last they decided to leave the ship, it was easy for them to reach the boat deck. In third class, leaving was next to impossible. There were only seven exits to the upper decks, and, because of the law, all were locked.

These third-class passengers could not easily find their way through the passageways by themselves. Many of them did not understand English and did not want to get into the boats. By the time they realized the ship was sinking, it was too late. At 1:40 A.M., two hours after the collision, an officer remembered that the steerage gates leading out of third class were still locked and he sent a steward to unlock them. The steward led groups of steerage passengers upward past the general meeting room on C deck, up a steep

Third-class passengers gazed at the fancy restaurant. They had never before seen such luxury.

emergency ladder, into first class, and out to the grand staircase which carried them to the boat deck. They passed by the first-class restaurant, the tables set with fine china, shining crystal, and polished silver, ready for the next day's breakfast. The steerage passengers had never seen such luxury, and they paused to gaze into the room in wonder, forgetting their fear for a moment.

It was hard to make them understand the emergency. When the steward reached the lifeboats and hurried them in, several women jumped out because they wanted to be back on the warm ship.

There were many more third-class passengers who could not find their way out at all. They perished. It was not because no one wanted to help them—there were just very few crewmen who could lead them out of the maze of corridors to the boat deck.

All the boats were gone by 2:00 A.M. and crewmen threw the last **collapsible boat** overboard. Men began to leap into the sea just as the sea water washed over the upper decks of the *Titanic*.

Passengers in the lifeboats looked back at the ship as they took the oars and rowed away. Some counted the rows of porthole lights and saw that the ship was getting lower in the water—five decks above water, then four, then three…lower and lower went the ship.

1:45 A.M. MONDAY, APRIL 15

As their lifeboat was lowered down to the water, Lottie saw the waves wash over the huge letters on the bow of the ship that spelled TITANIC. It looked as if the hungry sea was getting ready to devour the ship whole.

The men at the oars rowed strongly away as the crew on deck lowered the next lifeboat.

Lottie sat between her mother and a woman holding a baby in her arms. Where

These two French brothers, Michel and Edmond Navratil, lost their father in the disaster.

was her father? Was he still on the ship? Her mother was silent with worry. She would not look back at the ship, but held her head in her hands, her eyes closed. It felt lonely here in a small boat away from the warm and solid *Titanic*.

When they were far enough away, Lottie saw a sight that made her feel afraid. The great ship had begun to tilt downwards and the lights on board blinked out. There was a roaring noise as though all the heavy furniture in a house had been thrown downstairs. She could see a black shape rising up high in the dark night, turning and rolling, then it disappeared beneath the waves. Most horrible of all, she could hear the cries of passengers who drifted about in the water calling for help, a long, steady wail of terror that for the rest of her life she would not forget. At last, there was only silence and the sound of oars splashing through the water.

Where was her father? Was he in the water with those others?

The rowers pulled hard at the oars, moving away from the scene, searching for lights over the water, searching for a ship to save them. All that

The Radio Telegraph

Guglielmo Marconi invented the radio telegraph. In 1901, he was able to signal across the Atlantic from a wireless transmitting station in Cornwall, England, to St. John's, Newfoundland, a distance of about 3,500 kilometres. The two radio telegraphers on board the *Titanic* who gave the CQD and SOS calls worked for the Marconi Company. They were Jack Phillips and Harold Bride.

Jack Phillips taps out the message that the *Titanic* is sinking. The telegraphers stayed at their post until just before the *Titanic* sank.

Lottie could see were the lights of the bright stars in the sky.

2:30 A.M. MONDAY, APRIL 15

Where was Eliza? Beth sat in her aunt's arms, wrapped in a blanket but shivering in the cold night air. She was trying to be brave, but she was so sad about her doll. She had left her in her bed and now she would be covered by water with no one to take care of her. She might be already lost and at the bottom of the ocean. There were women in the lifeboat who were still wearing sparkling jewellery and wrapped in fur coats. One of them turned to Beth and wrapped a feather boa around her to help keep her warm. Little children on the boat were crying, but Beth knew she must be brave. She couldn't see the ship anymore—there was flat ocean where the *Titanic* used to be. She could hear sounds of screaming. "They're only singing to keep their spirits up," said her aunt, but Beth knew these were sounds of people in trouble.

A woman beside her, wearing a long evening gown, held a bundle in her arms.

Children of the Titanic

"Is that your baby?" she asked the lady.

The woman chuckled. "This is my little pet."

She opened the blankets to show Beth a toy pig. Its nose was missing and its legs were broken because someone had thrown it into the lifeboat. The lady twisted its tail and a bouncy little song played. She wrapped the blanket around Beth and let her pull on the pig's tail. Some children stopped crying when they heard the tinkling music.

"We will be safe," the woman told Beth. "My pig is my good luck charm."

Where were the boats?

There were twenty lifeboats on the *Titanic*, and four collapsible boats. There was room on them for less than half of all the passengers. Safety regulations in those days did not state that there had to be enough lifeboats to carry all the passengers and crew.

4:00 A.M. MONDAY, APRIL 15

"Take my coat," said John to a woman with a crying baby. The woman took it gratefully, and John sat huddled into his seat. He could feel a puddle of ice-cold water lapping over his feet and see his breath in the night air. They had been in the lifeboat for hours, everyone searching for lights on the ocean that would mean a ship was near. There was nothing to eat or drink.

John could scarcely bear to think about his father. It hurt to wonder about how much danger he was in. Was he floundering in the water with those others? When the ship had gone down, the cries and shouts for help were terrible to hear. In that first hour, people on the boat had argued about which direction they should row.

S   Sun deck
A   Upper promenade deck
B   Promenade deck, glass enclosed
C   Upper deck
D   Saloon deck
E   Main deck

F   Middle deck
G   Lower deck - cargo, coal bunkers,
    boilers, engines
    (a) Welin davits with lifeboats
    (b) Bilge
    (c) Double bottom

Very few third-class passengers were able to find their way out of the maze of corridors to the lifeboats.

Children of the Titanic

"We must row back! There are survivors!" one man called.

There was a confusion of voices, "Yes, we have room for more!" and "No! They will overturn us, there are too many in the water!"

John sided with those who wanted to go back. Of course, they must return. His father could be out there trying to stay alive, but John's voice was lost in the arguments.

There were many empty seats in his boat, room for at least twenty.

They took a vote. How many for going back? Yes, or no? The vote was cast. No. They would go onward toward their own rescue. Then everyone had become silent, too cold and miserable to speak.

John shifted seats with an exhausted rower, and took an oar along with someone else. They both heaved on the oar together and he felt gradually warmer. Other people took their turns at the oars as the long hours of darkness went on, or sat in a shivering doze, huddled down to stay warm.

Suddenly, from across the water, there came the

Some lifeboats left with many empty seats, but they did not go back to help save more people from drowning.

boom of a cannon and the shipwrecked passengers were startled out of their gloom. The man at the tiller shouted, "Ship ahoy!" John could see the lights of a big ship on the horizon. He thought it was just the stars, but then others sighted the ship and all their spirits leaped. John joined in with the rest, shouting, "Help us!" over and over.

It *was* a ship, and it loomed larger as they watched. Was it coming for them?

Children of the Titanic

CHAPTER SIX

Rescue at Sea

A flash of light. A faint boom. These were the first signals to the survivors that a ship was on its way. The "CQD" distress call from the *Titanic* had been picked up by several ships in the area, but the RMS *Carpathia* was closest, just ninety-three kilometres away. The liner headed north toward the *Titanic*'s last known

The very last message sent from the *Titanic*: "We are sinking fast. Passengers being put into boats."

location. Galley staff prepared hot drinks and meals. **Purser**'s staff prepared blankets and found empty berths. Lifeboats were swung out, poised for rescue. Rope ladders, cradle chairs for children—all were ready.

The ship's captain, Arthur Rostron, saw towering icebergs through the gloom, and carefully steered around them. Calls of "Icebergs to **port**," and "Icebergs to starboard," kept everyone's attention focused until the command "Full stop!" as an enormous iceberg floated straight ahead. The sun was beginning to rise, and an amazing sight met their eyes. In the pink glow of the rising sun, at least twenty monstrous icebergs floated among a stretch of field ice.

Captain Rostron could see a boat bobbing on the waves a short distance away. It looked as though the people in the boat were all covered in white frost, but as it drifted closer, he could see it was the white of their life jackets.

The captain edged his ship closer and sent men down to the gangway to help guide it alongside. Crew lowered the rope ladder and rings for the men and

Children of the Titanic

From a distance, the *Titanic* survivors' white life jackets made it seem as though they were covered with frost.

women, slings and cradles for the children and elderly. *Titanic* survivors, shivering with cold, climbed stiffly up the ladders and those watching from the *Carpathia*'s deck noticed how strangely they were dressed—in night dresses, dressing gowns, evening gowns, cloaks, and shawls. At last Captain Rostron heard the terrible news. The *Titanic* had sunk. At least a thousand people were lost.

4:45 A.M. MONDAY, APRIL 15

Hands were lifting Beth up into a cradle and she was swinging upwards and over the railing of the rescue ship. Aunt Sara was next, perched in the sling seat and tied to a life line that helped her to ascend.

Crowds of people stood on the upper decks, looking down at them in shocked silence. A crewman threw a blanket around Beth and picked her up. "We'll get some hot soup into your little girl," he said to Sara.

Beth saw the lady with the toy pig. A crewman was leading her, along with another group of women wearing fur wraps, up a staircase.

Beth and her aunt were led in a different direction, down below decks to a room in the hold. There, Beth recognized many of the women who had been with them in steerage. Some were dressed in their night

Children of the Titanic

Shocked survivors comfort each other on the deck of the *Carpathia*.

clothes and wrapped with ship's blankets. They looked up hopefully as Beth and her bedraggled group entered, searching for the familiar faces of their loved ones. Not many spoke English, and a crewman tried to make himself understood.

"What is your name? How much money do you have? Do you have friends in America?" he asked each person.

At a long table was a line of soup bowls and a steward came around with a steaming pot and ladled out the hot soup.

Beth and her aunt sat at the table with others, and Aunt Sara rubbed Beth's hands to warm them.

"I must send a cable to Beth's mother," said Aunt Sara.

"Do you have money with you?" asked the crewman.

A man beside them said he had only a dollar.

"Only one word for a dollar," said the crewman.

The man wrote "Saved" and gave his mother's address to the crewman.

Sara rummaged in her pocketbook. "I have only five dollars. Will that be enough?"

"One dollar for each word," said the man. "Give me your message and I will make sure it is sent."

Sara did as he asked, and wrote "Saved. Beth well." and gave him a few of her coins. She hoped the message would reach Beth's mother so that she wouldn't worry.

5:00 A.M. MONDAY, APRIL 15

When she had first seen the lights on the water, Lottie felt for certain it was just the stars, but then the lights

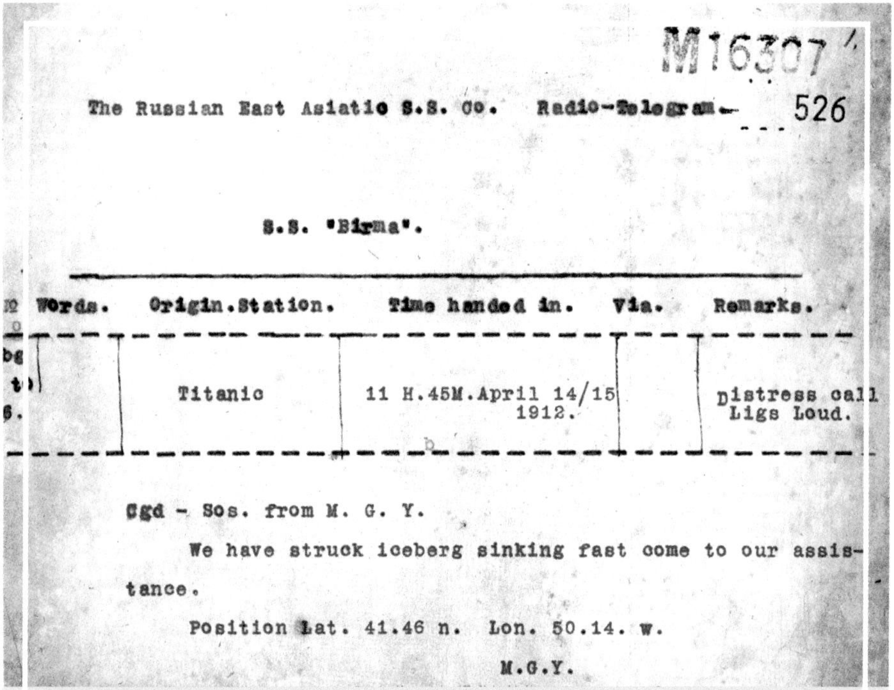

The Russian East Asiatic S.S. Co.   Radio-Telegram.

M 16307

526

S.S. "Birma".

Words.	Origin.Station.	Time handed in.	Via.	Remarks.
bg t) 6.	Titanic	11 H.45M.April 14/15 1912.		Distress call Ligs Loud.

Cgd - Sos. from M. G. Y.

We have struck iceberg sinking fast come to our assis-tance.

Position Lat. 41.46 n. Lon. 50.14. w.

M.G.Y.

The Heroes

Many crewmen stayed at their posts until long after it was safe to do so. Among these were the engineers down in the boiler rooms, who knew before anyone else that the ship was sinking. Jack Phillips and Harold Bride, radio telegraphers, stayed in the ship's office transmitting their calls for help until the very last moment before the ship sank. Jack Phillips died of hypothermia from being submerged too long in icy water, but Harold Bride survived. Pictured above is the last message that Jack Phillips sent.

The lifeboats of the *Titanic* were fastened to the *Carpathia*'s sides after the rescue.

had grown larger, and rockets were fired. It was a ship! Her mother sat up from her slumped position and hugged Lottie tightly as she gazed at the *Carpathia*. They could see other lifeboats in the water nearby and passengers being hauled up to the ship's deck.

The sun was just beginning to rise, and they seemed to be in a field of ice. Bergs rose out of the ice-packed water like the sails of yachts, their sides pink and glowing in the early morning sun.

Children of the Titanic

"Do you see Daddy?" Lottie asked her mother as the boat came closer to the ship. They looked up at the crowds of people on the deck who gazed down at them, and searched for him.

The boat gently bumped the side of the small ship and a sling was lowered, ready for Lottie. Her mother helped take off her life jacket. Then, as Lottie sat in the sling, a familiar voice called down to them.

"Is that my little girl? Lottie, Mary, is it you?"

Lottie's father stared anxiously down from the crowd of people on deck. He had found space on a lifeboat when no more women and children came forward.

"We're here. We're safe," called Lottie's mother from the boat and Lottie could hear the tears in her voice as she helped Lottie sit in the sling. Then Lottie was lifted upward and into her father's arms.

6:00 A.M. MONDAY, APRIL 15

John helped the women and small children out of their life jackets and into the sling or onto the rope ladder passed over the *Carpathia*'s sides.

A voice called over the side. "Where's my boy? Ned, are you down there?"

It was not his own father's voice, and John scanned the faces of those who watched from the deck above, survivors and passengers together, looking for his father.

"Here I am," shouted a voice.

Titanic **survivors on board the deck of** *Carpathia* **were helped and comforted by other passengers.**

Children of the Titanic

The boy who had disguised himself as a girl threw off his hat and shawl and jumped up. No one had discovered his disguise and there was some surprise among the passengers in the boat, and even some laughter. It felt good to laugh after such a terrible night. But John could not see his own father and when he was helped up the ladder and led, shivering, into the warm and comfortable lounge, there was still no sign of him, though John searched everywhere and asked each person he met, the crewmen and the rescued.

The decks of the *Carpathia* looked like a campground as exhausted people huddled here and there in blankets and borrowed clothes, and John looked carefully at every face. And when the last boat load of people was hauled up, John was there at the side of the ship, looking down and scanning the faces of the survivors, but his father was not among them, and John walked broken-hearted toward his cabin. There, he lay on his bunk and turned his face to the wall.

Epilogue

The *Carpathia* took on board all of the survivors in the lifeboats, then steamed toward the last reported location for the *Titanic*. All they found were small pieces of broken wreckage spreading for miles in the sea and only one body. By the morning of Wednesday, April

Newspaper reporters did not yet have all the facts about the tragedy.

16th, newspapers were reporting the unbelievable news. The *Titanic* had sunk and more than 1,500 passengers and crew were missing. On Thursday, April 18th, the *Carpathia* docked at Pier 54 in New York City to find 30,000 people waiting at the

Children of the Titanic

Tales of Heroism

There are many stories of heroic deeds performed by passengers and crew. Mr. Isidor Straus, first-class passenger, helped to bring women and children to the lifeboats and would not board the last lifeboat while there were others still to be saved. His wife refused to leave her husband's side no matter how much he begged her to get into a boat, and the two went down with the ship. The crew of the *Titanic* put their passengers' lives before their own, staying on board to save as many as they could before they themselves lost their lives. John Astor, the richest man on board, made sure his new bride was safe, but refused to board a lifeboat. He also went down with the ship.

dockside—relatives and friends of the survivors, mourners of those lost, and curious strangers.

9:40 P.M. THURSDAY, APRIL 18

The reporter had been waiting for the *Carpathia* for hours. He was at the front of the crowd and in a good position to get a story. The ship had just sailed up to the wharf and there was an excited buzz among the waiting crowds. The gangplank was lowered and all of those waiting surged against the roped-off area, pushing the reporter forward. The

The New York Times.

TITANIC SINKS FOUR HOURS AFTER HITTING ICEBERG;
866 RESCUED BY CARPATHIA, PROBABLY 1250 PERISH;
ISMAY SAFE, MRS. ASTOR MAYBE, NOTED NAMES MISSING

The Lost Titanic Being Towed Out of Belfast Harbor.

The tragedy made newspaper headlines around the world.
Reporters knew it was the story of the century.

Carpathia passengers came off the ship first, and the reporters waited for the *Titanic* survivors. Then they appeared. The first group of survivors walked down the gangway, dressed in clothes that did not fit, or wrapped in ship's blankets cut into ill-fitting coats, searching for relatives or friends in the crowd.

The reporter waved some dollar bills and shouted questions to the survivors as flash bulbs exploded in their faces. Waiting relatives wept and consoled one another, craning for a glimpse of their loved ones.

A young woman came down the gangway, holding a little girl in her arms who stared about her with large, frightened eyes. The woman ignored the reporter's questions and walked on.

A boy wearing a coat that was too big seemed lost in his own thoughts. The reporter opened his mouth to talk to him, but something about the boy's expression made him hesitate. An elegantly dressed woman in the crowd called out to the boy, and he turned at the sound of her voice. His mother, no doubt, thought the reporter. He left the two to their grief.

The Titanic begins its maiden voyage from Southhampton, England. Its story has now become legend and will always be remembered. April 2012 is the one-hundredth anniversary of the ship's tragedy.

Here came a family of three: father, mother, and young daughter. "Ten dollars for your story," he yelled, but they hardly noticed him as they walked by, their arms wrapped tightly around each other, sharing some private happiness of their own.

Seventy-three years later

The RMS *Titanic* was not lost forever in the ocean deeps. In 1985, Dr. Robert Ballard located the wreck, in two pieces, embedded fifteen metres into the sea bed. A self-propelled robot set off inside to explore the interior and found only echoes of the great ship. Photographs showed that the woodwork of the grand stairway was gone, eaten away by ocean brine, but the glass and crystal chandeliers hung

You might enjoy these books about the *Titanic*:

Finding the Titanic
by Robert D. Ballard

On Board the Titanic: What it was like when the great liner sank
by Shelley Tanaka

Polar, the Titanic Bear
by Daisy C. Speeden

That Fatal Night
by Sarah Ellis

White Star: A Dog on the Titanic
by Marty Crisp

SOS Titanic
by Eve Bunting

unchanged, and up in the crow's nest, the telephone line swayed in the current. It was a stark reminder of the grim message that had changed the lives of some 2,200 people on board: "Iceberg right ahead!"

Finding the *Titanic* Wreck

In 1985, scientist Dr. Robert Ballard and his team used a small, deep-sea submarine and sonar equipment to search for the RMS *Titanic*. They descended four kilometres to the sea floor where the wreck lay, six hundred kilometres southeast of Newfoundland. Ballard analyzed some steel taken from the hull. It showed a tendency for the metal to become brittle in very low temperatures, making it unsafe. When the ship collided with the iceberg, the ocean was -2°C. The steel plates buckled and the rivets came out, opening up gaps that let in the sea water. When the ship was built, this metal was the best available but would be considered very unsafe today.

Children of the Titanic

Acknowledgements

The author thanks Jonathan Walford, Curator, Fashion History Museum, Cambridge, Ontario; Charles Chambers, Curator, The Vina Cooke Museum, U.K.; Randy Bigham of the Randy Bryan Bigham Collection, Texas; Richard Rachals, Lunenburg, Nova Scotia; and finally, Kate Kennedy, Editor, for shepherding my words.

Image Credits

Archives of Ontario, used with permission of Sears Canada: 36.

Randy Bigham: 42.

Nova Scotia Archives: 6, 16, 19, 39, 44, 61, 69, 74, 76,

Richard Rachals: 52.

Sinking of the Titanic (1912): 9, 11, 20, 24, 48, 51, 71, 108,

Titanic Historical Society, Inc.: 2, 3, 4, 13, 14, 18, 22, 23, 28, 32, 58, 73.

Vina Cook Museum: 7.

Wikipedia Commons: 55, 60.

Woods Hole Oceanographic Institute: 84.

Glossary

Aft:	the back of the ship
Berth:	a bunk bed
Boat deck:	the deck on which the lifeboats are stored
Boiler:	a furnace where coal was burned to boil water that in turn created steam to turn the turbines that propelled a ship
Bow:	the front of a ship
Bridge:	the place at the front of a ship where the captain navigates
Coal:	brownish-black pieces of sedimentary rock used as fuel
Collapsible boat:	lifeboat with canvas sides that could be raised or lowered for use or storage
CQD:	a distress call in Morse code meaning "Seek You – Distress" or "All stations – Distress."
Crow's nest:	a lookout point on a ship's mast
Firemen:	see *stokers*
Fore:	toward the front

Funnel:	a ship's tall chimney that lets smoke and steam escape
Galley:	the kitchen on a ship or boat
Growlers:	bits of ice that have broken away from icebergs and that have air trapped inside them. As they melt, the escaping air makes a growling sound.
Helmsman:	the person who steers a ship or boat
Hull:	the main body of the ship
Marconi, Guglielmo:	born in 1874, an Italian scientist known for inventing the radio telegraph system
Parlour suite:	sitting room and bedrooms with connecting doors
Pneumatic tubes:	a system of cylinders and tubes to transport important papers or money short distances. The cylinders are pushed through pipes by the force of compressed air, or partial vacuum.

Children of the Titanic

Port:	the left-hand side of a ship as you face the bow
Promenade:	a deck where passengers can walk
Purser:	the person who looks after money matters and also the comfort of passengers on a ship
Quoits:	a deck game played with rope rings
SOS:	distress call sent using three dots, three dashes, three dots in Morse code
Starboard:	the right-hand side of the ship
Stateroom:	luxurious first-class bedroom on a ship
Steerage:	third-class cabins, the cheapest in the ship, located on the lowest deck above the boiler rooms
Stern:	the back of the ship
Stewards:	crew members who take care of passengers on a ship
Stokers:	crewmen who shovelled coal into the ship's furnaces

Telegram:	(from the Greek *tele*—far, *gram*—writing) a message sent or received over a long distance by a radio signal and using Morse code. Before long-distance telephone was invented, telegrams were the only way to send or receive messages over a long distance. Also called a "marconigram."
Tender:	a boat used to service a ship anchored out from shore. It carries passengers or cargo from shore to ship when the water is too shallow for the ship to sail into port.
Turkish bath:	a steam bath

Children of the Titanic

Index

Index